This book belongs to

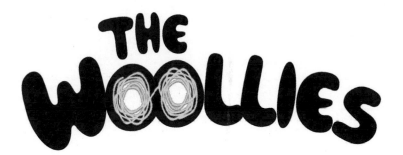

and

For my own expert imagi-knitters, Holly and Freddie xx—K.M^cK.
To my woollie consultants Harry, Ellie and Meggie—J.S.

OXFORD
UNIVERSITY PRESS

Great Clarendon Street, Oxford OX2 6DP

Oxford University Press is a department of the University of Oxford.
It furthers the University's objective of excellence in research, scholarship,
and education by publishing worldwide.

Oxford is a registered trade mark of Oxford University Press in the UK and in
certain other countries

Text © Oxford University Press 2018
Illustrations © Jon Stuart 2018

The moral rights of the author/illustrator have been asserted Database right
Oxford University Press (maker)

First published in 2018

British Library Cataloguing in Publication Data
Data available

ISBN: 978-0-19-274784-6 (paperback)

10 9 8 7 6 5 4 3 2 1

Printed in China

Paper used in the production of this book is a natural, recyclableproduct made
from wood grown in sustainable forests.The manufacturing process conforms to
the environmental regulations of the country of origin.

THE WOOLLIES

Follow the Footprints

Kelly McKain
Jon Stuart

OXFORD
UNIVERSITY PRESS

The Woollies were snoozing by their house.
Baby Woolly woke up first and . . .
'Look, Zip!' he cried. 'Footprints!'

'Who left them?' asked Zip.
'I don't know,' said Baby Woolly.
'Let's follow them!'

'Good idea!' said Zip. 'And can we make our own footprints too?'
'Yes,' said Baby Woolly.
'Let's imagi-knit!'

'Monster feet for making monster footprints!' said Baby Woolly.

Off they went,
following the footprints,
and making their own.
'Tramp, tramp, tramp!'
sang Zip.

Meanwhile, back at the Woollies'
house, Puzzle and Bling woke up.
'Where have Baby Woolly and
Zip gone?' they cried.

'Look, a terrible monster has
been here!' cried Bling.
'It's taken our Woollies away!' said Puzzle.
'We must rescue them. Quick,
it's time to imagi-knit!'

'All aboard the monster catcher!' cried Puzzle.
'Let's go and rescue Baby Woolly and Zip.'

'We're following the footprints –
footprints, footprints!
To catch the scary monster –
monster, monster!' Puzzle sang bravely.
Bling sang along, but not quite
so bravely.

Zip and Baby Woolly
were still following . . .

and following . . .

and following . . .

the footprints.

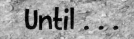

Until . . .

'Look!' said Baby Woolly.
'They were puppy prints!'
'I think he's trying to
find his bone,' said Zip.

'He needs our help,' said Baby Woolly.
'Ready, steady, imagi-knit!'

'Our dig-o-matic machine!' said Zip proudly.
They dug and dug and dug until, suddenly,
the puppy's bone was found.

'Wooooah!' wailed Baby Woolly.
'Help! Help!' shouted Zip.

Puzzle and Bling heard lots of
odd noises coming from the hole.
They rushed over to look.
They saw lots of strange feet.
'The monster!' Bling gasped.
'It's taken Baby Woolly and Zip
underground!' said Puzzle.

'Quick! Start the monster catcher!'
said Bling.

'Oh! But the monster is . . .

. . . Zip and Baby Woolly!' cried Puzzle.

'Then where is the real monster?' asked Bling.

'There is no real monster,' said Zip.
'It was us! We made the footprints!'

'Us and a puppy!' added Baby Woolly.
'Phew!' said Bling.
'What an adventure!' cried Puzzle.

'I'm tired now!' yawned Baby Woolly.
'Nap-time for baby monsters!'

A note for grown-ups

Oxford Owl is a FREE and easy-to-use website packed with support and advice about everything to do with reading.

Informative videos

Hints, tips and fun activities

Top tips from top writers for reading with your child

Help with choosing picture books

For this expert advice and much, much more about how children learn to read and how to keep them reading ...

LOOK
for Oxford Owl
www.oxfordowl.co.uk